AF186774

Klaus Kliem

English For Beginners

Grammar Lyrics Stories Tales

Na naszą korzyść - Nikomu nie szkodząc
Uns zum Nutzen – Niemandem zum Schaden

Alle in diesem Buch geschilderten Handlungen und Personen sind frei erfunden. Ähnlichkeiten mit lebenden oder verstorbenen Personen sowie anderen Publikationen sind nicht beabsichtigt und wären rein zufällig.

Die Deutsche Nationalbibliothek verzeichnet diese Publikation in der Deutschen Nationalbibliografie. Detaillierte bibliografische Daten sind über www.dnb.de
abrufbar.

Erste Auflage

Herstellung und Verlag BoD Books on Demand, Norderstedt

Palatino Linotype

ISBN 9783746056968

Inhalt - Grammar

Inhalt – Lyrics Stories Tales

Zeitformen

Zeitform	Signal-wörter	Verwen-dung	Bildung	Beispiele
Simple Present	every day sometimes always, often usually, seldom, never	regelmäßig wiederholte, gewohnheits-mäßige Handlungen	Infinitiv bei he/she/it + -s	I work he works I read he reads
Present Progressive	now at the moment look! listen!	Handlung geschieht im Moment des Sprechens	to be + Infinitiv + -ing	I'm working he's working I'm reading he's reading
Simple Past	Last … … ago, in 2017 yesterday	Handlung wurde in der Vergangenheit begonnen und abgeschlossen	regelmäßig: Infinitiv+ -ed unregelmäßig: siehe Verben	I worked he worked I came he came
Past Progressive	while	Handlung, die stattfand, als ein neues Ereignis eintrat	was/were + Infinitiv + -ing	I was working he was working I was reading he was reading
Simple Present Perfect	Just, yet never, ever already, so far up to now (since, for, recently)	Resultat einer Handlung, der Zeitpunkt ist uninteressant	have/has + past participle	I've worked he's worked I've read he's read
Present Perfect Progressive	all day, the whole day, how long, since, for	wie Simple Present Perfect aber mit besonderer Betonung des Ablaufs	have/has + been + Infinitiv + -ing	I've been working he's been working I've been reading he's been reading

Simple Past Perfect	already, just, never	Handlung, die vor einem bestimmten Zeitpunkt in der Vergangenheit angefangen haben aber darüber hinaus andauert	had + past participle	I had worked he had worked I had read he had read
Past Perfect Progressive	how long, since, for	Handlung begann vor bestimmten Zeitpunkt in Vergangenheit und dauert bis zu diesem oder darüber hinaus an	had + been + Infinitiv +-ing	I had been working he had been working I had been going he had been going
will -Future		Vorhersage künftiger Handlungen	will + Infinitiv	I'll work he'll work I'll read he'll read
going to - Future		bestehende Absicht / Plan	be + going to + Infinitiv	I'm going to work he's going to work I'm going to read he's going to read
Future Progressive		Handlung, die zu einem bestimmten Zeitpunkt in der Zukunft sein wird und bereits begonnen hat	will + be + Infinitiv +-ing	I'll be working he'll be working I'll be going he'll be going
Future Perfect Simple		Handlung, zu einem Zeitpunkt in der Zukunft abgeschlossen	will + have + past participle	I'll have worked, he'll have worked, I'll have gone, he'll have gone

Future Perfect Progressive		Handlung, zu einem Zeitpunkt in der Zukunft abgeschlossen mit beosnderer Betonung des Verlaufs	will + have + been + Infinitiv + -ing	I'll have been working, he'll have been working, I'll have been going, he'll have been going
Conditional Simple		Handlung tritt **vielleicht** ein, Typ II	would + Infinitiv	I would work, he would work, I would go, he would go
Conditional Progressive		Handlung, die **vielleicht** eintreten kann, mit Betonung des Verlaufs	would + be + Infinitiv +-ing	I would be working, he would be working, I would be going, he woul be going
Conditional Perfect		Handlung kann nicht mehr eintreten, zu spät, Typ III	would + have + past participle	I would have worked, he would have worked, I would have gone, he would have gone
Conditional Perfect Progressive		Handlung kann nicht mehr eintreten, zu spät, Betonung des Verlaufs	Would + have + been + Infinitiv +-ing	I would have been working, he would have been working, I would have been going, he would have been going

Das Konditional

Das **NULL KONDITIONAL** wird verwendet, wenn man sich auf eine jetzt oder immer gültige Zeit und eine reale und mögliche Situation bezieht.

	If -Satz	Hauptsatz
Bildung	If + Präsens	Präsens
Beispiel	If it rains	the street gets wet

Das **KONDITIONAL I** beschreibt eine wahre Situation in der Gegenwart oder Zukunft.

	If -Satz	Hauptsatz
Bildung	If + Präsens	Futur I
Beispiel	If it rains today	the street will get wet

Das **KONDITIONAL II** beschreibt irreale Situationen in der Gegenwart oder irgendwann.

	If -Satz	Hauptsatz
Bildung	If + Perfect (Simple Past)	Present Conditional oder Present Continuous Conditional
Beispiel	If it rained	the street would get wet

Das **KONDITIONAL III** beschreibt irreale Situationen in der Vergangenheit.

	If -Satz	Hauptsatz
Bildung	If + Past Perfect	Perfect Conditional oder Perfect Continous Conditinal
Beispiel	If it had rained	the street would have gotten wet

Das **GEMISCHTE KONDITIONAL** beschreibt Situationen in der Vergangenheit, die in der Gegenwart andauern.

	If -Satz	Hauptsatz
Bildung	If + Past Perfect oder Simple Past	Present Conditional oder Perfect Conditional
Beispiel	If we had worked harder	we would have better jobs now

Personalpronomen und Possessivpronomen

Personalpronomen		Possessivbegleiter	Possessivpronomen
als Subjekt	als Objekt	als Adjektiv	als Substantiv
I	me	my	mine
You	You	Your	Yours
he	him	his	his
she	her	her	hers
it	it	its	its
we	us	our	ours
You	You	Your	Yours
they	them	their	theirs
We have some books	The book is for **us**	These are **our** books	The books are **ours**
Wir haben einige Bücher	Die Bücher sind für **uns**	Das sind **unsere** Bücher	Die Bücher sind **unsere**
we ist Subjekt	**us** ist Objekt	**our** steht als Possessivbegleiter vor dem Substantiv	**ours** ist Substantiv

Reflexivpronomen

Personalpronomen	Reflexivpronomen
I	myself
you	yourself
he	himself
she	herself
it	itself
we	ourselves
you	yourselves
they	themselves

Relativpronomen

Das Relativpronomen erfüllt im Englischen und Deutschen die gleiche Funktion:
Seine Aufgabe ist es, die nähere Bestimmung eines Satzteils einzuleiten.

who → *der/die/das* und wird **bei Personen** eingesetzt
which → *der/die/das* und wird **bei Sachen und Tieren** eingesetzt
whose → *dessen* und wird **bei Personen, Sachen und Tieren** eingesetzt
Man benutzt für **who/which** auch manchmal **that.**

The man who lives here	Der Mann, der hier lebt
The boy who plays on the street	Der Junge, der auf der Strasse spielt
The bank which/that has all the money	Die Bank, die das ganze Geld hat
The trees which/that grow here	Die Bäume, die hier wachsen

Relativpronomen im Genitiv

The boy, whose bike was stolen has cried	Der Junge, dessen Fahrrad gestohlen wurde
The neighbour, whose wife died	Der Nachbar, dessen Frau gestorben ist
The computer, whose keybord is damaged	Der Computr, dessen Tastatur kaputt ist
The firm, whose employees have been fired	Die Firma, deren Angestellten gekündigt wurden

Relativpronomen im Dativ und Akkusativ

The man, whom I met yesterday	Der Mann, den ich gestern traf
The woman, to whom I sold my car	Die Frau, der ich mein Auto verkauft habe
The man, whom I love	Der Mann, den ich liebe

Whom kann man auch weglassen, nicht aber bei **all, both, each, either, many, neither, none, some**

The man I met yesterday	Der Mann, den ich gestern traf
The man I love	Der Mann, den ich liebe

Präpositionen

Präpositionen der ZEIT

Englisch	Deutsch	Verwendung	Beispiel
on	am	Wochentage	on Sunday
in	im in	Monate Jahrszahlen	in September in 2017
at	in am um	Tageszeiten am Wochenende konkrete Uhrzeit	at night at the weekend at nine
since	seit	ein Zeitpunkt	since 1999
for	seit	ein Zeitraum	for 8 years
ago	vor	ein Zeitpunkt in der Vergangenheit	11 years ago
before	vor	vor einem Zeitpunkt in der vergangenheit	before 2017
to	vor	bei Zeitangaben	two to two (13:58)
past	nach	bei Zeitangaben	Two past two (14:02)
to/till/untill	bis	bei von … bis …	From Saturday to/till/untill Monday
till/untill	bis	i. S. von wie lange etwas dauert	we have holiday till/untill Friday
by	bis	i. S. von spätestens bis zu einem bestimmten Zeitpunkt	they´ll be back by 10:15 pm by 10:15 they´ll have to do

space for Your notes

13

Präpositionen der RICHTUNG, der POSITION

Englisch	Deutsch	Verwendung	Beispiel
in	in auf	Raum, Stadt, Land Buch, Zeitung	in the kitchen, in London, in a car
at	an bei auf bei in	i.S. von daneben, davor, dabei, bei einem Ereignis, am Tisch, Ort, an dem man ist.	at the door, at the table, at a concert
on	an auf in	Befestigt, an einem Fluß, auf einer Etage	on the river, on the first floor
by, next to, beside	neben	daneben	standing next to ...
under	unter	unter etwas	under the table
below	unter	unter etwas	below the surface
over	über	wenn etw. bedeckt ist, und i.S. von mehr als	put a jacket over your shirt
above	über	oberhab	a path above the lake
across	über durch	auf die andere Seite gelangen	walk across the street
through	durch	Begrenzung d. Raumes	through the tunnel
to	zu nach in	zu einer Person, in einen Ort, ins Bett gehen	go to the party, go to Dublin, go to bed
into	in	in einen Raum, Gebäude hinein	go into the bathroom
towards	zu ... hinein	in Richtung	go 5 steps towards the building
onto	auf	auf etwas hinauf	climb onto the wall
from	von aus	von einem Ort	a letter from Glasgow
from	von	von einem Verursacher	a postcard from Mary

of	von	entspr. dem dt. Genitiv	the book of Mary
by	von	der Verursacher, Autor	a novel by Lord Byron
on	zu in	Reisen zu Fuß, zu Pferd, mit dem Bus	travel on foot, get on the bus
in	in	einsteigen in ein Auto, Zug	get in the car, train
off	aus	aussteigen aus dem Auto, dem Zug	get off the car, the train
out of	aus	aussteigen aus dem Auto, dem Zug	get out of the car, the train
by	um mit	Steigerung, Senkung, reisen mit dem Auto, Bus	prices have risen by12%, by car, by bus
at	mit	Altersangaben	he learned German at 5
about	über	i.S. von worüber	we are talking about her

Fragepronomen

Wer?	Who?
Was?	What?
Wie?	How?
Wo?	Where?
Warum?	Why?
Welche?	Which?
Wann?	When?

space for Your notes

Wortbildung

Suffixe Wie wird aus einem Verb ein Substantiv? Man hängt ein Suffix an das Verb.

Verb	Substantiv
to confirm	confirmation
to book	booking
to invent	invention
to act	actor
To move	movement
to drive	driver
to mean	meaning

Auch um aus einem Substantiv ein Adjektiv zu machen, wird ein SUFFIX angehängt.

Substantiv	Adjektiv
beauty	beautiful
fun	funny
industry	industrial
hope	hopeful/hopeless

Präfixe - Wie im Deutschen werden auch im Englischen mithilfe von PRÄFIXEN die **Negativformen von Adjektiven** gebildet.

Zu diesen Vorsilben gehören *un-, in-, im-* und *non-*.

happy	unhappy	efficient	inefficient
friendly	unfriendly	possible	impossible
necessary	unnecessary	perfect	imperfect
popular	unpopular	electric	nonelectric
correct	incorrect	essential	nonessential
tolerant	intolerant	violent	nonviolent
accurate	inaccurate		

Um die **Negativform von Verben** zu bilden, werden häufig die Vorsilben *mis-* und *dis-* benutzt.

to behave	misbehave	to agree	disagree
to place	misplace	to connect	disconnect
to understand	misunderstand	to like	dislike
to govern	misgovern	to appear	disappear

Modalverben

Modalverben sind **can, could, may, might, must, ought to, shall, should, will, would** und **need** (need kann auch normales Verb sein), **be, have** und **do** können **Hilfsverben und Vollverben** sein.

We can play football.	Wir können Fußball spielen.
We could play football.	Wir konnten Fußball spielen.
We may play football.	Wir dürfen Fußball spielen.
We might play football.	Wir könnten sogar Fußball spielen.
We must play football.	Wir müssen Fußball spielen.
We mustn't play football.	Wir dürfen nicht Fußball spielen.
We needn't play football.	Wir brauchen nicht/müssen nicht Fußball spielen.
We ought to play football.	Wir sollten Fußball spielen.
We shall play football.	Wir sollen Fußball spielen.
We should play football.	Wir sollten Fußball spielen.
We will play football.	Wir werden Fußball spielen.
We would play football.	Wir würden Fußball spielen.

Langform, bejaht	Kurzform, bejaht	Langform, verneint	Kurzform, verneint
can	--	cannot	can't
could	--	could not	couldn't
may	--	may not	--
might	--	might not	--
ought to	--	ought not to	oughtn't to
need	--	need not	needn't
shall	'll	shall not	shan't
should	'd	should not	shouldn't
will	'll	will not	wo
would	'd	would not	wouldn´t

Konjugation von „to be"

Present

I am
you are
he/she/it is
we are
you are
they are

Present Continuous

I am being
you are being
he/she/it is being
we are being
you are being
they are being

Simple past

I was
youwere
 he/she/it was
we were
you were
they were

Past Continuous

I was being
you werre being
he/she/is was being
we were being
you were being
they were being

Present perfect

I have been
you have been
he/she/it has been
we have been
you have been
they have been

Present Perfect Continuous

I have been being
you have been being
he/she/it has been being
we have been being
you have been being
they have been being

Past perfect

I had been
you had been
he/she/it had been
we had been
you had been
they had been

Past Perfect Continuous

I had been being
you had been being
he/she/it had been being
we had been being
you hade been being
they had been being

Future

I will be
you will be
he/she/it will be
we will be
you will be
they will be

Future Continuous

I will be being
you will be being
he/she/it will be being
we will be being
you will be being
they will be being

Future perfect

I will have been
you will have been
he/she/it will have been
we will have been
you will have been
they will have been

Future Perfect Continuous

I will have been being
you will have been being
he/she/it will have been being
we will have been being
you will have been being
they will have been being

Conditional
Conditional present

I would be
you would be
he/she/it would be
we would be
you would be
they would be

Conditional Present Progressive

I would be being
you would be being
he/she/it would be being
we would be being
you would be being
they would be being

Conditional perfect

I would have been
you would have been
he/she/it would have been
we would have been
you would have been
they would have been

Conditional Perfect Progressive

I would have been being
you would have been being
he/she/it would have been being
we would have been being
you would have been being
they would have been being

Subjunctive

Present subjunctive	Past Subjunctive	Past Perfect Subjunctive
I be	I were	I had been
you be; beest	you were; wert	you had been
he/she/it be	he/she/it were	he/she/it had been
we be	we were	we had been
you be	you were	you had been
they be	they were	they had been

Imperative

Participle

Imperative	Present Participle	Past Participle
you: be	being	been
we: let´s be		
you: be		

Das Gerundium

Das Gerund (oder auch Gerundium) ist ein Substantiv, das von einem Verb abgeleitet ist (substantiviertes Verb). Es wird gebildet mit Infinitiv + -ing

Das Gerundium **als Subjekt**: Going to parties is fun. (Auf Partys zu gehen macht Spaß.)

Das Gerundium als **Objekt**: I enjoy reading. (Ich mag es,zu lesen.)

Man übersetzt das Gerund ins Deutsche oft mit dem erweiterten Infinitiv mit zu oder auch einem Nebensatz. Verwechsle das Gerund nicht mit einer Progressive Zeitform.

Nach folgenden Verben darf nur das Gerundium stehen

admit He admitted having driven too fast. (Er gab zu, zu schnell gefahren zu sein.)

avoid They avoid going on holiday on Saturdays. (Sie vermeiden, an Samtagen in den Urlaub zu fahren.)

carry on If we carry on sleeping so badly, we may need help. (Wenn wir weiter so schlecht schlafen, werden wir Hilfe brauchen.)

consider Ralph is considering buying a new house. (Ralph denkt darüber nach, ein neues Haus zu kaufen.)

delay I delayed telling Max the news. (Ich verschob es, Max die Neuigkeiten zu erzählen.)

deny She denies reading the book. (Sie lehnt es ab, das Buch zu lesen.)

dislike We dislike reading poems. (Wir mögen das Lesen von Gedichten nicht./ Wir mögen es nicht, Gedichte zu lesen.)

can't/couldn't help He couldn't help falling in love with her. (Er konnte nicht anders, als sich in sie zu verlieben.)

enjoy I enjoy playing chess. (Ich genieße es, Schach zu spielen.)

finish They finished working in the garden. (Sie haben aufgehört, im Garten zu arbeiten.)

give up Susan gives up playing ice-hockey. (Susan gibt das Eishockeyspielen auf.)

imagine He imagined driving a new car. (Er stellte sich vor, ein neues Auto zu fahren.)

include Your responsibility includes taking reservations on the phone. (Deine Aufgabe beinhaltet, Reservierungen am Telefon entgegenzunehmen.)

involve The project will involve growing plants. (Das Projekt wird auch Pflanzenanbau betreffen.)

justify I cannot justify paying $100 for this ticket. (Ich kann es nicht rechtfertigen, 100 Dollar für die Eintrittskarte zu bezahlen.)

keep (on) They keep on running. (Sie rennen/laufen weiter.)

mention Did Alex ever mention playing baseball? (Hat Alex schon erwähnt, dass er Baseball spielt?)

mind I don't mind sleeping on the couch. (Ich habe nichts dagegen, auf der Couch zu schlafen.)

miss They miss playing with their friends. (Sie vermissen es, mit ihren Freunden zu spielen.)

practise She practised playing hockey. (Sie trainierte das Hockeyspielen.)

regret* Do you regret having mentioned it? (Bedauerst du, das erwähnt zu haben?)

risk You risk catching a cold. (Du riskierst, dich zu erkälten.)

suggest She suggested flying to Cairo. (Sie schlug vor, nach Kairo zu fliegen.)

*Nach **regret** kann auch der Infinitiv mit to folgen (meist mit einer negativen Nachricht verbunden).We regret to inform you that the flight to Berlin has been cancelled.

Nach bestimmten Wendungen steht das Gerundium

to be busy He is busy reading the paper. (Er ist gerade dabei, die Zeitung zu lesen.)

don't mind I don't mind telling them my opinion. (Es macht mir nichts aus, ihnen meine Meinung zu sagen.)

feel like We feel like having a cup of tea. (Uns ist nach einer Tasse Tee.)

how about How about walking home instead of taking the car? (Wie wäre es mit Heimlaufen, statt mit dem Auto zu fahren?)

it's (no) good It's no good talking to this girl. (Es hat keinen Zweck, mit dem Mädchen zu reden.)

it's no use It's no use talking to the headmaster. (Es hat keinen Sinn, mit dem Schulleiter zu sprechen.)

spend one's time They spend their time reading. (Sie verbringen ihre Zeit mit Lesen.)

there's no There's no cheating anymore. (Es gibt kein Mogeln mehr.)

there's no point There's no point in complaining further. (Es ist zwecklos, sich weiter zu beschweren.)

what about What about going to the zoo? (Wie wäre es mit einem Zoobesuch?)

worth The book is worth reading. (Es lohnt sich, das Buch zu lesen.)

Aktiv – Passiv

Für das Vollverb wird immer die Partizip-Form benutzt. Vor dem Verb steht im Passivsatz immer eine Form von (to) be, (to) have oder will be/going to (je nachdem in welcher Zeit der Aktivsatz steht). Diese Form steht in der gleichen Zeit wie das Verb im Aktivsatz.

Simple Present	I use a pen	The pen is used by me
Present Progressive	I am using a pen right now	A pen is being used by me
Simple Past	I used a pen yesterday	A pen was used by me yesterday
Past Progressive	I was using a pen yesterday	A pen was being used by me yesterday
Present Perfect	I have used a pen once	A pen has been used by me for a week.
Present Perfect Progressive	I have been using a pen since August	A pen has been being used by me
Past Perfect	I had used a pen before I bought a pencil	A pen had been used by me
Past Perfect Progressive	I had been using a pen for a month when it broke	A pen had been being used by me
Future I Simple (will)	I will use a pen tomorrow	A pen will be used by me
Future I Progressive (will)	I will be using a pen at the exam	A pen will be being used by me at the exam

Future I Simple (going to)	I am going to use a pen at the exam	A pen is going to be used by me at the exam
Future I Progressive (going to)	I am going to be using a pen at the exam	A pen is going to be being used by me
Future II Simple (will)	I will have used a pen when I come back	A pen will have been used by me
Future II Progressive (will)	I will have been using a pen for two hours when the exam ends	A pen will have been being used by me for 2 hours when the exam ends
Future II Simple (going to) **selten**	I am going to have used a pen when I come back	A pen is going to have been used by me
Future II Progressive (going to) **selten**	I am going to have been using a pen	A pen is going to have been being used by me

Space for Your notes

23

Redewendungen

blind wie ein Maulwurf	as blind as a bat
grinsen wie ein Honigkuchenpferd	to grin like a Cheshire cat
wie ein Elefant im Porzellanladen benehmen	to behave like a bull in a china shop
brüllen wie am Spieß	cry blue murder
dumm wie Bohnenstroh	as dumb as a post
jemandem ein X für ein U vormachen	to lead someone up the garden path
die Flinte ins Korn werfen	to throw in the towel
noch grün hinter den Ohren sein	to be half-baked
zwei Fliegen mit einer Klappe schlagen	to kill two birds with one stone
in den sauren Apfel beißen	swallow the bitter pill
aus dem Schneider sein	be out of the woods
den Wald vor lauter Bäumen nicht sehen	see the forest for the trees
um den heißen Brei reden	beat about the bush
sich den Mund fusselig reden	talk until one is blue in the face
mehrere Eisen im Feuer haben	to have two strings to one's bow
den Braten riechen	smell a rat
Blut und Wasser schwitzen	to be in a cold sweat
übers Ohr hauen	pull a fast one
kein Blatt vor den Mund nehmen	not to mince matters
die Nase voll haben	be fed up
übers Knie brechen	rush one's fences
auf großem Fuß leben	live like a lord
klar wie Kloßbrühe	as sure as eggs is eggs

24

auf die hohe Kante legen	save up for a rainy day
auf Herz und Nieren prüfen	put something to the acid test
die Katze im Sack kaufen	buy a pig in a poke
über den eigenen Schatten springen	bite the bullet
die zweite Geige spielen	take a back seat
ein Machtwort sprechen	put one's foot down
auf dem falschen Dampfer sein	bark up the wrong tree
zwei linke Hände haben	fingers like toes
aus dem Nähkästchen plaudern	give away secrets
mit Kind und Kegel	everything but the kitchen sink
Äpfel mit Birnen vergleichen	compare apples and oranges
das Kind beim Namen nennen	call a spade a spade
die Radieschen von unten ansehen	be six feet under
die Radieschen von unten ansehen	be pushing up the daisies
ins Gras beißen	kick the bucket
in den Sand setzen	muck something up
den Bach runtergehen	go to hell in a handbasket
Löcher in den Bauch fragen	pester someone with questions
aus einer Mücke einen Elefanten machen	make a mountain out of a molehill
mit dem ist nicht gut Kirschen essen	It's best not to tangle with him
auf dem Holzweg sein	to be on the wrong track
etwas im Keim ersticken	nip in the bud
Schnee von gestern sein	water under the bridge
sich auf die Socken machen	take to one's heel

jemanden über den grünen Klee loben	to praise to the skies
etwas im Schilde führen	to have something up one's sleeve
ein Esel schimpft den andern Langohr	the pot calls the kettle black
alle Wege führen nach Rom	all roads lead to Rome
Aller guten Dinge sind drei	Third time is a charm
Alte Liebe rostet nicht	old flame never dies
Alter schützt vor Torheit nicht	There's no fool like an old fool
Auge um Auge, Zahn um Zahn	tit for tat

Besser ein Spatz in der Hand als eine Taube auf dem Dach
                                  a bird in the hand is worth two in the bush

Der Apfel fällt nicht weit vom Stamm	the apple does not fall far from the tree
Der Appetit kommt beim Essen	appetite comes with eating
Der frühe Vogel fängt den Wurm	the early bird catches the worm
Der Zweck heiligt die Mittel	the end justifies the means
Die Katze beißt sich in den Schwanz	vicious circle
Die Schönheit liegt im Auge des Betrachters	Beauty is in the eye of the beholder
Die Würfel sind gefallen	the dice is cast
Ein Unglück kommt selten allein	It never rains but it pours
eine Hand wäscht die andere	one hand washes the other
Eine Schwalbe macht noch keinen Sommer	one swallow doesn't make a summer
einem geschenkten Gaul schaut man nicht ins Maul	Don't look a gift horse in the mouth
Ende gut, alles gut	All's well that ends well
Es ist nicht alles Gold, was glänzt	All that glitters is not gold
Gleich und Gleich gesellt sich gern	Birds of a feather flock together

gut Ding will Weile haben	good things are worth waiting for
Hochmut kommt vor dem Fall	pride goes/comes before a fall
Hunde, die bellen, beißen nicht	barking dogs seldom bite
Jeder ist seines Glückes Schmied	Every man is the architect of his own fortune
Kindermund tut Wahrheit kund	children are never shy about telling the truth
Lügen haben kurze Beine	a lie has no legs
Man muss das Eisen schmieden, solange es heiß ist	make hay while the sun shines
Morgen, morgen, nur nicht heute, sagen alle faulen Leute	don't put off for tomorrow what you can do today
Morgenstund hat Gold im Mund	The early bird catches the worm
Pünktlichkeit ist die Höflichkeit der Könige	Punctuality is the politeness of kings
Reden ist Silber, Schweigen ist Gold	Speech is silver, but silence is golden
Steter Tropfen höhlt den Stein	Constant dripping wears the stone
Stille Wasser sind tief	Still waters run deep
Unter den Blinden ist der Einäugige König	Among the blind the one-eyed is king
Unwissenheit schützt vor Strafe nicht	ignorance of the law is no excuse
viele Köche verderben den Brei	Too many cooks spoil the broth
Was du heute kannst besorgen, das verschiebe nicht auf morgen	1) a stitch in time saves nine 2) there's no time like the present
Was sich liebt, das neckt sich	the quarrel of lovers is the renewal of love
Wenn man vom Teufel spricht, kommt er	Speak of the devil, and he will appear
Wer A sagt, muss auch B sagen	in for a penny, in for a pound
Wer anderen eine Grube gräbt, fällt selbst hinein	harm set, harm get
wer nicht wagt, der nicht gewinnt	Nothing ventured, nothing gained

Wer Wind sät, wird Sturm ernten	Sow the wind, reap the whirlwind
Wer zuerst kommt, mahlt zuerst	First come, first served
Wie gewonnen, so zerronnen	Easy come, easy go
Wie man in den Wald hineinruft, so schallt es heraus	What goes around, comes around
Wo ein Wille ist, ist auch ein Weg	where there's a will there's a way
Wo gehobelt wird, fallen Späne	you can't make an omelette without breaking eggs
Zeit ist Geld	time is money
Übung macht den Meister	Practice makes perfect
sichmit Ach und Krach den Sieg erkämpfen	scramble a victory
Von schönen Worten kann man nichts kaufen	Fine words butter no parsnips
mit der Tür ins Haus fallen	go like a bull at a gate
wenn Ostern und Pfingsten auf einen Tag fallen	when hell freezes over
sich um Kopf und Kragen reden	risk one's neck with careless talk
mit Lob geizen	be sparing with one's praise

space for Your notes

28

The Prince And The Pauper

by Mark Twain

Chapter I.

The birth of the Prince and the Pauper

In the ancient city of London, on a certain autumn day in the second quarter of the sixteenth century, a boy was born to a poor family of the name of Canty, who did not want him. On the same day another English child was born to a rich family of the name of Tudor, who did want him. All England wanted him too. England had so longed for him, and hoped for him, and prayed God for him, that, now that he was really come, the people went nearly mad for joy. Mere acquaintances hugged and kissed each other and cried. Everybody took a holiday, and high and low, rich and poor, feasted and danced and sang, and got very mellow; and they kept this up for days and nights together. By day, London was a sight to see, with gay banners waving from every balcony and housetop, and splendid pageants marching along. By night, it was again a sight to see, with its great bonfires at every corner, and its troops of revellers making merry around them. There was no talk in all England but of the new baby, Edward Tudor, Prince of Wales, who lay lapped in silks and satins, unconscious of all this fuss, and not knowing that great lords and ladies were tending him and watching over him--and not caring, either. But there was no talk about the other baby, Tom Canty, lapped in his poor rags, except among the family of paupers whom he had just come to trouble with his presence.

I Wandered Lonely as a Cloud

By William Wordsworth

I wandered lonely as a cloud
That floats on high o'er vales and hills,
When all at once I saw a crowd,
A host, of golden daffodils;
Beside the lake, beneath the trees,
Fluttering and dancing in the breeze.

Continuous as the stars that shine
And twinkle on the milky way,
They stretched in never-ending line
Along the margin of a bay:
Ten thousand saw I at a glance,
Tossing their heads in sprightly dance.

The waves beside them danced; but they
Out-did the sparkling waves in glee:
A poet could not but be gay,
In such a jocund company:
I gazed—and gazed—but little thought
What wealth the show to me had brought:

For oft, when on my couch I lie
In vacant or in pensive mood,
They flash upon that inward eye
Which is the bliss of solitude;
And then my heart with pleasure fills,
And dances with the daffodils

Streets Of London

Ralph McTell - Miscellaneous

Have you seen the old man in the closed down market
Kicking up the paper with his worn out shoes
In his eyes you see no pride
Hand held loosely by his side,
yesterday's paper telling yesterday's news
How can you tell me you're lonely
And say, for you, that the sun don't shine
Let me take you by the hand
And lead you through the streets of London
I'll show you something to make you change your mind

Have you seen the old gal who walks the streets of London
Dirt in her hair and her clothes in rags
She's no time for talkin, she just keeps right on walkin
Carryin her home in two big shopping bags
In the all night cafe at a quarter past eleven
Same old man sitting there on his own
Looking at the world over the rim of his teacup
Each tea lasts an hour and he goes home alone

Have you seen the old man outside the seaman's mission
Memory fading like the ribbons that he wears
In our winter city, the rain cries a little pity
For one more forgotten hero in a world that doesn't care

For Limericks

Anonymous

There was a young Lady in Niger
Who smiled as she rode on a tiger
They returned from the ride
With the Lady inside
And the smile on the face of the tiger

There once was a man from Peru
Who had a lot of growing up to do
He'd ring a doorbell
Then run like hell
Until the owner shot him with a 22

A bather whose clothing was strewed
By winds that left her quite nude
Saw a men come along
And unless we are wrong
You expected this line to be lewd

There was an old man with a beard
Who said, 'It is just as I feared!
Two Owls and a Hen,
Four Larks and a Wren,
Have all built their nests in my beard!'

Problems of Immigrants

In some parts of Britain there are still problems between immigrants and white people today. Here Ali Zafri from Liverpool is talking about some problems: "Like many other people from Pakistan we came to Britain in 1967. Pakistan is a poor country and the British government promised us jobs and houses. When I first came to Liverpool with my wife, I found a job in a factory. Today we've got a small shop. Life isn't always easy for Asian people. When we arrived we felt that white people didn't accept us as British, but there were lots of jobs for us in the factories. During the last ten years things have become worse. Lots of people are out of work now and some people think we steal their jobs. Some of them even hate us. Last week some white hooligans beat some Asian children in our street. Some of my friends are returning to Pakistan because they don't feel safe in Britain now, but I've decided to stay because Liverpool has become my home.

Coco

One day Jack Stone and his new friend Mike went home together. Jack wanted to show Mike Coco, his parrot. When Jack was at school he kept the bird in a big cage, but in the afternoon Coco could fly around in his room. Jack liked the bird very much, because it was so clever and learned to speak quickly. It could imitate his father's voice so that Jack's mother sometimes answered from the kitchen, because she thought it was Mr Stone. When the boys arrived at the house a police car was waiting in front of it. Two policemen were coming out. They were taking a man to the police station. "Something very strange has happened,"

Mrs Stone said to the boys. "The police have arrested a dangerous thief, but nobody seems to know who called them." When Jack opened the door of his room a minute later a loud voice was shouting: "Catch the thief!", and Coco was jumping around in the cage in front of the open window.

Child labour in Britain in the 19th century

Between 1700 and 1830 the English industry grew very fast. England became the most important industrial country in the world. To make more money the managers of the factories and mines began to employ children and women. Unfortunately the machines in those days weren't very safe. Many of them worked with steam and the children had to climb into the machines to clean oil parts that no adult could reach. They had to work for more than twelve hours a day and sometimes they fell into the machines. For this reason most factories had a stopper. He was a kind of a guardian. He walked around the factory and awoke up the children when he saw them falling asleep at their work.

Penfriends

Rick would like to write to somebody of his own age in Germany. A month ago he wrote to a magazine with all his hobbies: playing football, riding on his bike, playing the guitar and watching car races on TV. His letter was printed and a few boys and girls have written to him. One boy says that although he is frightened of flying he flies to Canada every summer with his family and goes climbing in the Rocky Mountains. He enjoys windsurfing, playing tennis and reading comics in his spare time.

The Three Sillies
English Folktale

Once upon a time there was a farmer and his wife who had one daughter, and she was courted by a gentleman. Every evening he used to come and see her, and stop to supper at the farmhouse, and the daughter used to be sent down into the cellar to draw the beer for supper. So one evening she had gone down to draw the beer, and she happened to look up at the ceiling while she was drawing, and she saw a mallet stuck in one of the beams. It must have been there a long, long time, but somehow or other she had never noticed it before, and she began a- thinking. And she thought it was very dangerous to have that mallet there, for she said to herself: "Suppose him and me was to be married, and we was to have a son, and he was to grow up to be a man, and come down into the cellar to draw the beer, like as I'm doing now, and the mallet was to fall on his head and kill him, what a dreadful thing it would be!" And she put down the candle and the jug, and sat herself down and began a-crying.

Well, they began to wonder upstairs how it was that she was so long drawing the beer, and her mother went down to see after her, and she found her sitting on the settle crying, and the beer running over the floor. "Why, whatever is the matter?" said her mother. "Oh, mother!" says she, "look at that horrid mallet! Suppose we was to be married, and was to have a son, and he was to grow up, and was to come down to the cellar to draw the beer, and the mallet was to fall on his head and kill him, what a dreadful thing it would be!" "Dear, dear! what a dreadful thing it would be!" said the mother, and she sat her down aside of the daughter and started a-crying too.

Then after a bit the father began to wonder that they didn't come back, and he went down into the cellar to look after them himself, and there they two sat a- crying, and the beer running all over the floor. "Whatever is the matter?" says he. "Why," says the mother, "look at that horrid mallet. Just suppose, if our daughter and her sweetheart was to be married, and was to have a son, and he was to grow up, and was to come down into the cellar to draw the beer, and the mallet was to fall on his head and kill him, what a dreadful thing it would be!" "Dear, dear, dear! so it would!" said the father, and he sat himself down aside of the other two, and started a-crying.

Now the gentleman got tired of stopping up in the kitchen by himself, and at last he went down into the cellar too, to see what they were after; and there they three sat a-crying side by side, and the beer running all over the floor. And he ran straight and turned the tap. Then he said: "Whatever are you three doing, sitting there crying, and letting the beer run all over the floor?"

"Oh!" says the father, "look at that horrid mallet! Suppose you and our daughter was to be married, and was to have a son, and he was to grow up, and was to come down into the cellar to draw the beer, and the mallet was to fall on his head and kill him!" And then they all started a-crying worse than before. But the gentleman burst out a- laughing, and reached up and pulled out the mallet, and then he said: "I've travelled many miles, and I never met three such big sillies as you three before; and now I shall start out on my travels again, and when I can find three bigger sillies than you three, then I'll come back and marry your daughter."So he wished them good-bye, and started off on his travels, and left them all crying because the girl had lost her sweetheart.

Well, he set out, and he travelled a long way, and at last he came to a woman's cottage that had some grass growing on the roof. And the woman was trying to get her cow to go up a ladder to the grass, and the poor thing durst not go. So the gentleman asked the woman what she was doing. "Why, lookye," she said, "look at all that beautiful grass. I'm going to get the cow on to the roof to eat it. She'll be quite safe, for I shall tie a string round her neck, and pass it down the chimney, and tie it to my wrist as I go about the house, so she can't fall off without my knowing it." "Oh, you poor silly!" said the gentleman, "you should cut the grass and throw it down to the cow!" But the woman thought it was easier to get the cow up the ladder than to get the grass down, so she pushed her and coaxed her and got her up, and tied a string round her neck, and passed it down the chimney, and fastened it to her own wrist. And the gentleman went on his way, but he hadn't gone far when the cow tumbled off the roof, and hung by the string tied round her neck, and it strangled her. And the weight of the cow tied to her wrist pulled the woman up the chimney, and she stuck fast half-way and was smothered in the soot.

Well, that was one big silly.

And the gentleman went on and on, and he went to an inn to stop the night, and they were so full at the inn that they had to put him in a double-bedded room, and another traveller was to sleep in the other bed. The other man was a very pleasant fellow, and they got very friendly together; but in the morning, when they were both getting up, the gentleman was surprised to see the other hang his trousers on the knobs of the chest of drawers and run across the room and try to jump into them, and he tried over and over again, and couldn't manage it; and the gentleman wondered whatever he was doing it for. At last he stopped and wiped his face with his handkerchief. "Oh dear," he says, "I do think trousers are the most awkwardest kind of clothes that ever were. I can't think who could have invented such things. It takes me the best part of an hour to get into mine every morning, and I get so hot! How do you manage yours?" So the gentleman burst out a-laughing, and showed him how to put them on; and he was very much obliged to him, and said he never should have thought of doing it that way.

So that was another big silly.

Then the gentleman went on his travels again; and he came to a village, and outside the village there was a pond, and round the pond was a crowd of people. And they had got rakes, and brooms, and pitchforks, reaching into the pond; and the gentleman asked what was the matter. "Why," they say, "matter enough! Moon's tumbled into the pond, and we can't rake her out anyhow!" So the gentleman burst out a-laughing, and told them to look up into the sky, and that it was only the shadow in the water. But they wouldn't listen to him, and abused him shamefully, and he got away as quick as he could.

So there was a whole lot of sillies bigger than them three sillies at home. So the gentleman turned back home again and married the farmer's daughter, and if they didn't live happy for ever after, that's nothing to do with you or me.

Human Rights Day is observed on December 10, every year in order to safeguard and protect the rights of common people. Now-a-days, more and more countries, states and local provinces celebrate this day due to so many ill practices that are prevalent across the globe. There can be such times, when you may be required to join a group that fights for human rights and you may be needed to give speech consequently.

Human Rights Day Speech

I would like to welcome everyone to the sixth annual celebration of Human Rights Day. Our NGO was established seven years ago with the purpose of protecting the rights of common people as well as supporting the poor and deserted people. For all those who are new to our NGO, I would brief about the background of Human Rights Day. Adopted in the year 1948 by the United Nations General Assembly, it is observed every year on December 10th by the international community. The day is usually marked by high-level political conferences & meetings as well as by cultural events and exhibitions which deal with the issues of human rights.

Our NGO is one of its kind in this district, thus we deal with all types of issues involving protecting and advocating human rights. Like every year, this year too, we will be working around one theme and this year's theme is 'Right to education'. This Right recognises right to free and compulsory primary education for everyone as well as a commitment & responsibility to develop secondary education available to all, especially through the introduction of secondary education free of cost and an obligation to expand equitable and impartial access to higher education, through development of free higher education.

Education is everyone's right and it is very critical especially for people staying in rural areas to understand the value of education. In most of the remote areas in our country, parents still feel that girl child is not required to study as they ultimately have to manage home. This is absolutely an unfair expectation as education makes girls stronger and helps them in taking decisions as well as managing home in a better way. It also gives them mental as well as intellectual strength to fight against the ill practices prevalent in our society, such as dowry torture, domestic violence and other crimes against women.

I am proud to share that our NGO has transformed around 100 such villages into more awakened places. With the help of donations received, we have opened primary, secondary as well as higher secondary schools in approximately 89 villages so far and are in the progress of making schools in the remaining 11villages.

We are getting enormous support and appreciation from several people especially youngsters in our mission. There are many youths, who impart free education involuntarily at these schools and it's a great beginning, I would say. We have also received the support of the state government for spreading awareness towards education in more and more villages and rural areas. Government has also promised us financial support in opening up schools in more and more villages.

Some Bad Jokes

Three Doughters

There once was Gary who was raising three daughters on his own. Gary was very concerned about their well being and always did his best to watch out for them. As they entered their late teens the girls dated, and on this particular evening all three of his girls were going out on a date. This was the first time this had occurred. As was his custom, Gary would greet the young suitor at the door holding his shotgun, not to menace or threaten but merely to ensure that the young boy knew who was boss.

The doorbell rang and the first of the boys arrived. Father answered the door and the guy said, "Hi, my name's Joe, I'm here for Flo. We're going to the show, is she ready to go?" The father looked him over and sent the kids on their way.

The next lad came and said, "My name's Eddie, I'm here for Betty, we're gonna get some spaghetti, is she ready?" Gary felt this one was okay too, so off the two kids went.

The final young boy arrived and Gary opened the door. The boy started off, "Hi, my name's Chuck, I am here for …" and Boom! Gary shot him.

Lipsticks

A middle school for girls was faced with a unique problem. A number of girls were beginning to use lipstick and would put it on in the bathroom. That was fine, but after they put on their lipstick they would press their lips to the mirrors leaving dozens of little lip prints.

Finally the principal decided that something had to be done. She called several of the girls to the bathroom and met them there with the custodian. She explained that all these lip prints were causing a major problem for the custodian who had to clean the mirrors every day.

To demonstrate how much work they were making for the custodian, she asked him to clean one of the mirrors while the girls watched. The custodian took a long-handled brush, dipped it into the nearest toilet, and proceeded to scrub the mirror.

From that day on, the problem of lip prints on the mirrors was completely eliminated.

As I Was Going To St. Ives

(A Math Riddle?)

As I was going to St Ives
I met a man with seven wives
Each wife had seven sacks
Each sack had seven cats
Each cat had seven kits
Kits, cats, sacks, wives
How many were going to St. Ives?

Romeo and Juliet Act 3, Scene 5
by William Shakespeare

Juliet   Wilt thou be gone? It is not yet near day.
           It was the nightingale, and not the lark,
           That pierced the fearful hollow of thine ear.
           Nightly she sings on yon pomegranate tree.
           Believe me, love, it was the nightingale.

Romeo It was the lark, the herald of the morn,
           No nightingale. Look, love, what envious streaks
           Do lace the severing clouds in yonder east.
           Night's candles are burnt out, and jocund day
           Stands tiptoe on the misty mountain tops.
           I must be gone and live, or stay and die.

Juliet   Yon light is not daylight, I know it, I.
           It is some meteor that the sun exhales
           To be to thee this night a torchbearer,
           And light thee on thy way to Mantua.
           Therefore stay yet. Thou need'st not to be gone.

Romeo Let me be ta'en. Let me be put to death.
           I am content, so thou wilt have it so.
           I'll say yon grey is not the morning's eye.
           'Tis but the pale reflex of Cynthia's brow.
           Nor that is not the lark, whose notes do beat
           The vaulty heaven so high above our heads.
           I have more care to stay than will to go.
           Come, death, and welcome! Juliet wills it so.—
           How is 't, my soul? Let's talk. It is not day.

Quotes
by Winston Churchill

United wishes and good will cannot overcome brute facts,'
Churchill wrote in his War Memoirs. 'Truth is incontrovertible.
Panic may resent it. Ignorance may deride it. Malice may distort it.
But there it is.

The inherent vice of capitalism is the unequal sharing of
blessings. The inherent virtue of Socialism is the equal
sharing of miseries.

One would have thought that if there was one cause in the
world which the Conservative party would have hastened
to defend, it would be the cause of the British Empire in
India ... Our fight is hard. It will also be long ... But win or
lose, we must do our duty. If the British people are to lose
their Indian Empire, they shall do so with their eyes open.

Danger gathers upon our path. We cannot afford – we have
no right – to look back. We must look forward

In the twinkling of an eye, I found myself without an office,
without a seat, without a party, and without an appendix.

It may seem strange that a great advance in the world   in
industry, in controls of all kinds, should be made in time of
war ... War has taught us to make these vast strides
forward towards a far more complete equalisation of the
parts to be played by men and women in society.

A gentleman does not have a ham sandwich without
mustard.